A COWBOY'S COOKBOOK

A COWBOY'S COOKBOOK

BY T. L. BUSH

WITH THE PHOTOGRAPHS OF ERWIN E. SMITH

★

TexasMonthlyPress

Photographs from the Erwin E. Smith Collection of Range Life Photographs, Library of Congress. All photographs used by permission.

Illustrations by Terry Toler

Texas Monthly Press, Inc.
P.O. Box 1569
Austin, Texas 78767

A B C D E F G H

Library of Congress Cataloging in Publication Data

Bush, T. L., 1947–
  A cowboy's cookbook.

  Includes index.
  1. Cookery (Beef)   I. Title
TX749.B86   1985   641.6′62   85-7967
ISBN 0-87719-011-9 (pbk.)

Design by Terry Toler

To my family and to the thousands of friends I've got all over the country—to them I say thanks. And to the handful of soreheads, I also say thanks, because if you hadn't been so damned spiteful I might not realize how important a friend is. And to all the kids that dream of being cowboys or cowgirls, I say keep on dreaming—you can make it happen. I did.

OR Ranch, Arizona. 1909–1910. *The OR outfit having dinner in the hot noonday sun.*

CONTENTS

Box T Ranch, Arizona. 1909–1910. *The wagon cook of the Box T in action while one of the cowhands comes in for a snack.*

INTRODUCTION

ᴊᴀ ꙭ ɴx ꓒ ⊶ # Ⓐ ᦄ ᴏx ⌁ ᦾ ⱬ

Cooking should be fun, not work. The urge to experiment and a desire to express one's creativity are all you need to relax from the everyday pressures of job and material hassles.

If you think cooking is standing in a kitchen with a cookbook and measuring utensils, you might just as well go buy pre-packaged convenience foods, because these foods are all premeasured to taste the same every time. I don't think that's cooking.

Shortly after buying a cookbook supposedly of true cowboy and western cooking, I hastily rewrapped the book and made a present of it to an acquaintance of which I was not particularly fond. I figured he deserved it. That book was full of ideas and ingredients no self-respecting cowboy or ranch cook could pronounce or cook with—let alone eat!

I want people to use this book as a guide, not as a step by step instruction manual. If you should encounter a recipe you would like to try but don't have one of the ingredients, don't dismiss it. "Cowboy-up," get tough, and substitute. Your results may be better than mine.

I hope you enjoy using this book as much as I enjoyed gathering and creating the recipes for you. In using this book, all you are really doing is experimenting. Always cook with three things in mind: taste, smell, and appearance.

Never be afraid to add something just to see how it will taste. That's the fun of cooking.

T. L. "Bull" Bush

Matador Ranch. *The chuck wagon followed by the hoodlum outfit.*

BEEF AND LAMB

ᴊᴀ ꝗ ɴх ꝗ ⊸ # ⊛ ⊂ ᴏх ⌐ ⊡ ᴢ

It's been said that all a cowboy thinks about is horses, cows, roping, riding, drinking, dogs, and women, not necessarily in that order. Now, I agree these things frequently cross every cowboy's mind but none of them are foremost in a cowboy's life. You may not believe it but the most important thing is eating. Cowboys are always talking about food. I've spent most of my life traveling or working with other cowboys and in everything we do we usually get around to eating or at least talking about it. Some examples I've heard:

Saddling up for work in the morning. "Hurry up and eat, horse, you're gettin' more for breakfast than I do."

Sale barn during a cattle sale. "Let's get something to eat while they're selling them canners and cutters."

Horse sale. "Hell, they'll sell tack till two. Let's get a sandwich."

Roping wild cows. "She'd look better cooked than on the end of my damned rope."

While riding through the pasture. "I wonder what's for dinner tonight. I'm hungry enough to eat this horse."

While drinkin' in a saloon after about six beers. "What they got to eat in here? I ain't eaten since last night, I'd better put something in my gut if I'm goin' to drink any more."

Working cattle with the dogs. "Eat 'er up dog, but save the good steaks for me."

Talkin' about women. "She might be a little 'brahmer-headed,' but damn, that woman can cook!"

Now, with this evidence I think I have proven that if you want to get a cowboy to do anything, just promise him something good to eat. I remember one day we were working

350 head of cattle for a feller—just so we could all go to a cookout and he wouldn't have to stay at home. After all, it was the bankers' cookout and we figured we had all paid for it several times over!

You know, I've found there are just about as many ways to ruin a good piece of meat as there are to make it good. You can take a nice cut of meat and make it taste bad, and you can make a bad cut of meat taste great by cooking it the right way.

The best meats for roasting or broiling come from the parts of the animal where the muscles are least used, i.e., T-bone, ribeye, sirloin, etc. You can develop a delicious flavor in these cuts with seasoning and care, while you roast or broil 'em.

Now the rest of the animal ain't bad. It just requires a little more care and preparation. Take roasts for example. There ain't anything much better than roast and potatoes. But first you need to rub flour on that roast and throw it into a hot skillet and sear it—that means you cook the outside real quick so you can lock in the flavor and prevent the escape of the natural juices. Then reduce the heat and let it all cook slowly. Otherwise the outside will become dry and hard before the heat can get down to the inside. The bigger the roast, the lower the heat.

If you don't use a covered cooker, be sure to baste that rascal a bunch with the natural juices in the pan. If you don't have a broiler, you can fake it. Just throw that rascal into a hot skillet with a little oil and brown both sides. Turn that heat way down and cook it slowly.

If you get a tough piece of meat, you might be able to soften it up a bit by using a meat mallet. If you don't have one, don't worry. Use something else, such as the back side of a knife or some other blunt object. I try to stay away from tenderizing products because most of them contain an acid of some kind that is designed to tear down the fiber in the meat. I don't know what it does to your stomach. A lot of fast food steak houses use this procedure and it sure don't get along with my innerds. A good heavy, covered skillet will do wonders for tenderizing a good sized roast.

ROAST BEEF

Once upon a time in a land that seems to be far, far away, I used to own a restaurant and we featured a buffet–type lunch and dinner. One of our specialties was roast round of beef. Here is the way I was taught to cook it:

Roast:
Whatever size roasting pan you need for the size roast you have.

Put meat in the pan, rub with flour and salt and pepper to your likin'.
A little garlic powder or salt ain't bad either.

Place in a hot oven around 500 degrees just to brown the meat. When browned, reduce to about 350 degrees.

If you want rare beef, figure about 15 minutes per pound starting after you get it browned.

For well done, allow 20 minutes per pound.

Be sure to baste it frequently with the natural juices in the pan.

If you are going to have a big get together, bring a nice top of round and cook it this way. Then slice it thin or "feather it," as they say. If you don't burn the hell out of it, they'll talk about your great dinner for years to come, I'll bet'cha!

CUTS OF BEEF

CHUCK
1. Beef for Stew, Ground Beef
2. Blade Roast, Boneless Chuck Eye Roast
3. Shoulder Post Roast, Arm Pot Roast, Brisket
4. Cross Rib Pot Roast

FORE SHANK

5. Shank Cross Cuts
6. Beef for Stew
7. Brisket

RIB, SHORT PLATE

8. Short Ribs, Ground Beef, Skirt Steak Rolls
9. Rib Roast, Rib Steak, Rib Eye—Roast or Steak

SHORT LOIN

10. Top Loin Steak, Porterhouse Steak, T-bone Steak
11. Boneless Top Loin Steak
12. Filet Mignon—Steak or Roast

FLANK

13. Ground Beef
14. Flank Steak

SIRLOIN

15. Pin Bone Sirloin Steak, Boneless Sirloin
16. Flat Bone Sirloin Steak
17. Wedge Bone Sirloin Steak
18. Boneless Sirloin Steak

ROUND, TIP

19. Rolled Rump
20. Round Steak, Cubed Steak, Bottom Round, Eye of Round
21. Tip Steak, Tip Roast
22. Heel of Round, Ground Beef

GRIZZLY BEER MEAT

One day I was sitting around the camp trying to figure out what I could fix to go with a batch of Indian fry bread (Saddlebag Bread) I was fixing. Well, I was listening to the radio and a country music singer started singing a song about how he liked beer. Seeing as how I couldn't argue the point, I decided to help keep them people at the brewery working, and have a beer and think this food thing over. Then it came to me! It's hard to go too wrong with hamburger and I knew everybody there liked beer so this is what resulted:

1½ lbs. hamburger

1 cup beer (more or less depends on how much beer you've got)

1 cup ketchup (cut back a little if you want, it's mostly sugar)

1 tablespoon vinegar

5 tablespoons what's-this-here-sauce (Worcestershire)

salt & pepper to taste

Mix all the ingredients in a large skillet, crumble in hamburger, and let simmer for about one hour.

This sure was good with that fry bread!

(Also known as "Saddlebag Bread" in this cookbook.)

Shoe Bar Ranch, Texas. 1901–1910. *A Shoe Bar wagon and some of the boys eating.*

BANDIT BURGERS

From time to time grocery stores will have a special on ground round. In my opinion, beef ground from any part of the critter can be made to taste good. Anyway, if you want to try some ground round for something special this makes a pretty good mess.

    2 lbs. ground round
    ¼ lb. mild pork sausage
    6 or 8 slices bacon
    1 cup tomato sauce
    parsley
    salt and pepper
    flour

Mix beef and sausage, salt and pepper to taste, shape into burgers, and roll them in the flour. Fry bacon till crisp, remove from pan, and keep bacon warm. Fry burgers in the bacon grease until brown and remove them from the skillet. Leave a small amount of drippings in the pan. Add the tomato sauce, stirring and mixing in the crumbles left from the burgers and bacon until well blended. When the sauce is good and hot, pour it over the burgers. Crumble and sprinkle the bacon and parsley over the burgers and sauce.

A CHUCKWAGON PRIMER

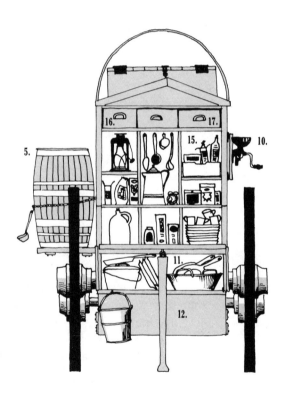

1. rifle
2. bows
3. keg of horseshoes
4. tarpaulin
5. water barrel
6. washtub
7. bedrolls
8. tool box
9. chuck box
10. coffee grinder
11. Dutch oven, pots and pans
12. boot
13. brake
14. lantern
15. foodstuffs (corn meal, flour, pinto beans, bacon, coffee, sugar, and salt)
16. first aid (castor oil, calomel, and bandages)
17. essentials (whiskey, chewing and rolling tobacco)

REAR VIEW

SIDE VIEW

BEEF'N'BEANS

When cowboys used to trail cattle from Texas, they were fed an awful lot of beans, basically because they were easy to keep. Well, the book wouldn't be complete if I didn't mention some easy bean fixing!

    ½ cup sliced onions
    1 can corned beef
    1 11 oz. can pork'n'beans
    5 or 6 slices bacon

Mix up everything except the bacon, then spoon it into a suitable casserole dish. Lay single strips of the bacon on top and bake at 350 degrees for 30 minutes.

POP'S VEGETABLE BEEF SOUP

It's usually not very hard to get cowboys to eat practically anything, vegetables included. The hard part is having enough veggies to go around. Here's one sure fire way to fill 'em up (at least for one meal).

2 lbs. hamburger
2 medium potatoes, diced
2 celery stalks, diced
1 medium onion, diced
1 16 oz. package frozen mixed vegetables, or fresh
1 can beef boullion
2 15 oz. cans tomato sauce
¼ head cabbage, chopped (small head)
1 teaspoon garlic salt
¼ teaspoon pepper
1 stick margarine
water

Brown and crumble hamburger. Drain well. In a five-quart kettle, melt one stick of margarine and sauté vegetables (fresh or frozen), celery, onion, and potatoes. When tender (fresh vegetables will be crisper), add hamburger and all remaining ingredients. Mix well. Add one to two quarts water (depends on quantity and thickness of the soup desired). Bring to a boil. Reduce heat and simmer for 1 hour, covered.

Matador ranch, Texas. 1909. *A Matador cook at the business end of a chuck wagon after the cowpunchers have had breakfast and gone for the day's work.*

OL' FOOLER

One of the ranches I used to work for had several thousand acres and a bunch of these acres was in timber. Now it seems one day we were moving a bunch of cows and calves out of a section of pasture and one ol' cow decided we were going the wrong direction and broke loose and took her calf to the timber. The foreman said rather than lose more cattle to the woods we would keep driving and come back to get her. After we got the other cattle moved he sent four of us back after momma and calf. Riding through that bunch of trees wasn't easy, but after awhile we found them. We all punched a hole in our ropes and the chase was on.

We ran under, around, and sometimes into what seemed to be every tree in the woods and finally we got 'em headed toward a big bluff. We knew we had 'em where we wanted, or so we thought. That calf came to a sliding stop at the edge, looked down that forty foot bank, and didn't like what he saw. Momma cow was a different story. She bailed off that bank and went rolling ass-over-appetite clear to the bottom, got up, shook herself off, and took off back into the brush! It was about weaning time so we roped the calf, made a halter out of a rope, and led him back to the trailer. To make a long story shorter, we chased that cow off and on for two months. In that time I saw that cow do things to avoid capture that cattle just ain't supposed to know how to do. Things like the time she lay down by a log until the two cowboys that were chasing her rode by. Or like the time she jumped in a ditch and hid. Then there was the time she hid in a bunch of brush until the cowboys got right beside her—then charged their horses bellering like a bull. She scared those cowboys and horses so bad both punchers got bucked off. Back into the timber she ran!

I swear that cow could climb trees. Well, one day all of us were mad at the old cow and a little embarrassed because word had got out we couldn't catch one little old cow, so all

15

twelve of us saddled up to go after her.

It was like a military attack meeting. We all agreed the best place to catch her would be at the forty foot bluff. So, while nine riders chased, the other three of us waited at the foot of the bluff. Sure as hell, here she came off over the edge, ass-over-appetite again, but this time when she hit bottom, there were three ropes on her so fast she didn't stand a chance! After a considerable fight we had her haltered and took turns dragging her back to a trailer, got her loaded, and decided we had better take her to one of the feed lot pens since they had tall board fences and she couldn't get out of them. I can't tell you how funny it was when we finally realized that twelve cowboys were at least smarter than one dumb old cow.

When we got her back to the pens there was a bunch of people gathered to see this cow that was so smart. It didn't take long for word of the capture to get around. I remember we backed up to the gate, unloaded the cow and watched in disbelief as she started to jump the fence, miscalculated the top board, fell over the fence and broke her damn fool neck and died right on the spot!

Now cowboys may be crazy but we're not all dumb. Quicker than quick we were over the fence and slit her throat to at least salvage the meat. Well, we hauled her one more

LS Ranch, near Tascosa, Texas. 1908. *The LS chuckwagon and boss on the move late in the evening.*

time, only we ended up at the locker plant where they processed her and divided the meat into twelve equal portions (more as a joke) for each of us!

Early the next spring just before calving, I had all the cowboys and their wives to our house for a feed. They each brought a covered dish and I cooked the meat. When the foreman and owner commented on how good the meat was and asked what it was, I told 'em, "Ol' Fooler," the cow we chased for two months last fall. That brought a smile to everyone's face and then a toast to the smartest cow any of us had ever known. Then one of the boys said "She wasn't too damn smart." When asked why, he said, "Well, hell, Bush finally caught her in a frying pan!" A lot of people think they have to go buy the most expensive cut of beef to serve to their friends. Folks, this just ain't so. This simple little recipe will melt in your mouth and not cost a bunch.

salt
1 egg (beaten)
cracker crumbs
2 lbs. round steak

Cut steak into individual servings. Salt to taste. Dip each piece in egg and then into cracker crumbs. Brown the meat on both sides in a hot skillet. Turn heat down to simmer and cover with water. Let cook about 2½ hours or until tender. I think your guests will like it.

CALF ROPER'S CASSEROLE

Most calf ropers will tell you the only thing a critter's flank is good for is to be used to throw one down with. Boy, are they wrong. Here is a dish that's darn good, considering what it's made of.

    1 flank steak
    salt & pepper to taste
    1 tablespoon minced onion
    1 tablespoon lemon juice
    1½ cup tomatoes
    1 cup crumbs
    1 pint hot water
    speck of nutmeg

Rub the salt, pepper, and nutmeg into steak. Roll up the steak and tie it with a string and sear it. Put it in a casserole dish, pour in the hot water, cover and bake at 325 degrees for about two hours or until tender. To thicken your juices, you could add a small can of tomato sauce and then serve while warm.

SUNDAY BEEF & PIG

This recipe has been tested by some of the most critical people in the world—the cowboys across the midwest and western United States. If something ain't good, they have a way of letting you know it!

    2 lbs. round steak
    ½ lb. bacon
    2½ cups water
    2–4 tablespoons flour
    salt & pepper

Salt and pepper steak to your liking. Lay strips of bacon on round steak, cut steak about the same width of the bacon. Roll bacon and steak strips together with bacon inside. Stick a toothpick through each roll to hold them together.

Brown meat in hot frying pan then put the meat in a baking dish. Pour water in frying pan and let it simmer awhile. Now slowly add a mixture of flour and water (approximately 2–4 tablespoons flour and 1 cup water) stirring constantly until the broth reaches the desired thickness. Pour this over the meat. Cook in the oven at 350 degrees for about 1 hour.

Shoe Bar Ranch, Texas. 1905–1910. *Shoe Bar chuck wagon, hoodlum wagon, and some of the boys in camp having dinner.*

BACHELOR BUTT

Even a single feller can fix this and maybe it will even help him land a wife!

>   2 lbs. rump roast
>   salt
>   pepper
>   butter
>   What's-this-here-sauce (Worcestershire to some)

Rub soft butter all over meat and salt and pepper to your liking and let it stand for awhile (go drink a beer or something). Now cut several deep gashes on the top and fill with Worcestershire. Put in a broiling pan and broil about 15 minutes, turn it over and cut some gashes in the other side, pour in more sauce and sprinkle some over the roast if you wish. Broil till done—rare.

If this doesn't have her thinking you are some catch, something ain't right in her mind or you screwed up dinner!

BULL-RIDER'S STEAK

Put a three pound steak—one and one half inches thick—in a shallow roaster and sear the meat on both sides in butter. Cover the steak with slices of onion, carrots, green peppers, and stuffed olives, adding the liquid from the olives, and one half pound fresh mushrooms, sliced. Add one can tomato sauce thinned with one half can water. Cook 1½ hours at 350 degrees. For the last 30 minutes, remove cover.

This steak will make any bullrider "hang in there" until the whistle, knowing he has this treat waiting for him at the end of the ride.

SMS range, Texas. 1908. *Cowpunchers sitting around the fire eating "son-of-a-bitch" (stew of livers, kidneys, etc.)*

CATTLEMAN'S SUNSET

Every once in awhile I like to do things a little fancy for my guests. I mean it ain't always barbecue, chili, or grilled hamburgers. I like to serve this on a nice clear fall evening just as the sun is going down. That's how it got its name.

ribeye or sirloin steak (about 1½ inches thick and enough to fill about four of
    your guests)
salt & pepper to taste
Worcestershire sauce
1½ lbs. fresh mushrooms
¾ cup cream
2 tablespoons butter
corn oil (olive oil if you like it)

Soak meat in mixture of oil, salt, pepper, and Worcestershire sauce for about 2½ hours. Brown meat on both sides and then broil, turning once. Slice mushrooms in half and cook in butter seasoned with salt and pepper and add cream. Place steak on a nice platter and cover with the mushroom sauce.

I like to cook some store-bought tater tots to serve with this steak.

WHISKEY STEW

This is another one of them things that just naturally seemed to happen. We were just sitting around shooting the bull and listening to cowboy songs when another feller drove up, yelled his hello to the camp, and we hollered back to "come on in." Much to our pleasure he had a friend of ours with him—you might know him—our friend's name is Jack Daniels. Well, our cowboy friend set Jack on the table, broke the seal and threw the cap away. With four cowboys and a bottle of libation just sitting there, we knew something would probably happen so I decided I'd finish fixing something to eat so that whiskey wouldn't have to be alone just sitting in our bellies. I was going to fry up some deer steaks but with our new guest I didn't quite have enough to go around so it was "stretch time." So, over a jug of whiskey and a hot stove we created Whiskey Stew.

2 lbs. deer steak (or beef round steak)

1 16 oz. can tomato sauce

1 16 oz. can of peas (do not drain)

1 10 oz. can of cheddar cheese soup

1 16 oz. can green beans (do not drain)

2 cups water

1 teaspoon smoke flavor (liquid smoke)

3 tablespoons molasses

2 tablespoons mustard

1 can refrigerator biscuits

2 shots whiskey

salt, pepper, Tabasco sauce to taste

deep fryer ½ full of lard (lard just seems to make things taste better)

While deep fryer is heating to hot, slice deer steak into bite size chunks. When lard is hot, drop steak chunks into fryer and cook until browned. Remove and place on a paper towel to drain. Reduce heat on the fryer to warm—we'll get back to it.

On a warm burner place a soup pot and add to it in this order: tomato sauce, green beans, water, smoke flavor, molasses, mustard, salt, pepper, and Tabasco sauce. Stir well, add one shot of whiskey—let it find its own way around the pot by not stirring. Cover and let it cook for 15 minutes. Next, add the meat and bring to a boil for another 15 minutes. Reduce the heat to medium again. Add peas and cheddar cheese soup. Stir, mixing soup in well. Cover for another 10 minutes.

Fire that fryer up, but not quite so hot this time. While this is happening, open the biscuits, place on a cutting board, mash them half flat, and with a sharp knife cut each biscuit into three pieces. Drop biscuit pieces into the hot lard and cook until they are just golden, not dark. Do not overload the fryer so the biscuits will have plenty of room, cook good, and not get soggy. Remove and place on paper to drain, then drop them in on top of the Whiskey Stew. Serve immediately.

I think just about everyone will like it. We did! Oh, and that second shot of whiskey, you might as well drink it as there ain't no use putting it in the stew. You couldn't taste it anyway!

JA Ranch, Texas. 1907. *The JA chuck wagon camped on Cotton Wood Creek.*

BUTT À LA BANKER

I was fed this barbecue while working for a short time on a ranch out in western Nebraska. The cook always seemed to enjoy serving this when the boss had a party and especially if the banker was invited. It seems the banker would always comment on how interesting the barbecue was until finally one day the cook told him, "No, that critter was part of the principal," and assured him the interest was alive and well and still grazing out on the range. That's why the cook named this barbecue, "Butt à la Banker."

Bake a 4 to 6 pound butt roast at 350 degrees for 1 hour per pound (25 minutes per pound in a microwave). Slice it thin and spread it out in a pan or casserole. Simmer this sauce about 30 minutes and pour it over the roast.

4 tablespoons chopped onion
½ teaspoon chili powder
½ teaspoon pepper
¼ teaspoon cinnamon
½ teaspoon salt
1 teaspoon paprika
½ teaspoon dry mustard
1 clove garlic, chopped
2 tablespoons Worcestershire sauce
3 tablespoons white vinegar
1 small can tomato sauce
½ can water (use tomato sauce can)

Now, put the whole mess back in the oven and continue baking at 350 degrees for another hour. Slap this on buns or serve over fried potatoes. It takes a pretty mean son-of-a-gun to not like this grub! Makes about 20 servings.

WHEN THERE'S NO HOPE

1–2 lbs. round steak (cut into bite sized pieces)
1½ cups flour
¼ cup cornmeal
garlic salt
pepper
vegetable oil

Mix flour and cornmeal. Coat each piece liberally with garlic salt and pepper then roll in flour and cornmeal mixture.

Put enough oil into a heavy fry pan to cover at least half of the meat and heat. When hot, drop coated steak into the oil and brown on each side. Remove and drain on paper towel. Pieces will be golden brown and crunchy and this takes only minutes to make when you think "there ain't no hope of pleasing 'em."

LS Ranch, Texas. 1907–1909. *Some LS cowboys riding along with the chuckwagon on the move.*

BUNCH QUITTER CASSEROLE

T his recipe came to me one day while we were driving about three hundred head of cattle down a five mile stretch of road while I was punchin' cows on the G-Bar. Now there's two big fears of driving cattle down a gravel road: First, is vehicles coming from the opposite direction at a high rate of speed. For this you use a man riding point or in front of the cattle checking for open gates, etc., and slowing down oncoming traffic.

Second, is "bunch quitters," or cattle that try to make their own trail and not stay with the bunch. For this you have cowboys riding flank, or alongside the herd.

Well, naturally it had to happen, and at the worst possible place. I was riding flank on an old pony called Tanglefoot. Now, he had trouble sometimes just walking and at this particular time he stumbled going clear down to his knees. While we were gathering ourselves up, this danged bunch quitter made her move and took three or four cows with her. Off the road they went, and right up through the Widow Story's garden, but that's where it ended because the garden was fenced, all but the side along the road. Before we could get those cows out of her garden, it looked like they had most of it plowed up. There were vegetables everywhere!

After everything was taken care of with the Widow Story, I asked Jim, the foreman, if he wouldn't like to have that cow on the end of his rope to control her. His reply, "Hell no, I'd rather have her mixed with all them vegetables and put in a pot!" That's how "Bunch Quitter Casserole" got its name.

Take a large greased baking dish and add to it in this order:

> 1 layer sliced onions
> 1 layer sliced potatoes
> 1 layer ground round steak or hamburger (put a little pork sausage in it if you want to, after all you're cooking it, not me)
> 1 layer sliced carrots
> 1 can kidney beans

Season each vegetable to taste as you fill the baking dish. Top it all with 1 can tomatoes. Bake slowly for 2 hours at 325 degrees.

JA Ranch, Texas. 1907. *Chuckwagon and hoodlum on the move followed by the remuda.*

OR Ranch, Arizona. 1910. *Jeff Milton (extreme left) on his dun-colored horse, and the Greene Cattle Company outfit getting ready to move.*

SALISBURY STEAK

My mamma would sometimes fix up some quick meals whenever I would manage to stop by their house when I used to run the roads. One of the things she used to fix was a Salisbury Steak type stuff. I always liked it and so did the cowboys traveling with me.

2 lbs. good ground beef
salt & pepper to taste
1½ teaspoons lemon juice
dash of nutmeg
1 egg
3 teaspoons minced onions
1 can tomato sauce

Mix all this stuff together except the tomato sauce and form mixture into individual burgers. Broil 'em until you think they are done enough—depends on how well done you like your beef. While that's cooking, warm that tomato sauce—don't boil it—just warm it. Put the burgers on a platter and pour that tomato sauce all around 'em. If you want to spice it up a bit, slice an onion and lay the rings on top.

CHILI

The other day I was messing around the homestead doing real important things like counting my socks, calling the time and temperature number on the phone, and listening to a talk show host interview a lawyer on the radio about people getting married. You know, real important stuff like that. Well, I knew I had some things that needed to be done outside like chopping ice or exercising my horse and I knew the last time I called the time and temperature number the recording told me to "Save energy, bank by mail." The time was 4:07 and the temperature was minus 10 with a wind chill of 22 degrees below, so I wasn't real excited about saddling that horse or busting no ice. So, I got scientific and democratic. I figured those horses were out of the wind and would not come out until the water had frozen again, so there was no need of breaking it in the first place. Then I stuck my head out the back door and shouted, "Horse, I'll be fair about this, if you want to go for a ride just say so and we'll go." You know, that horse never said a thing and never even stuck his head out of the barn! With my second problem solved it was back to important matters such as what to fix to eat.

As I passed the radio on my way to the freezer, I heard this lawyer still talking about his "see, see plan for newlyweds." I didn't know if he was talking about a little "show and tell" before marriage, or a trip to Mexico for the honeymoon. But, as my dad told me, "If you'd shut up and listen you might find out," so I did and it wasn't either. His plan was to see your lawyer before you see your preacher. Well the humor wasn't much but hearing the see, see made me think of South Texas and Mexico and I knew it was going to be Mexican cooking tonight!

Not having all the ingredients for my favorite home fixed chili, and I knew I didn't want to drive to town to get them, I decided to try some quick chili from what I had on hand. These are just what I had. You might want to substitute or add to it.

1½ lbs. ground beef
1 lb. deer burger
1 pint home-canned tomatoes
1 pint home-canned tomato juice
1 16 oz. can pork'n'beans (I didn't have chili beans)
1 15 oz. can tomato sauce
1 teaspoon salt
1 teaspoon crushed red pepper
6 tablespoons chili powder
pinch of garlic salt (it was there, so I used it)
black pepper to taste

Mix everything (except the meat) together in a big pot. Stir it all up and cook at medium high heat until it comes to a boil, then reduce heat to medium, stirring occasionally. Crumble and brown meat in skillet, drain off grease, and add meat to sauce. Cook combined ingredients for 30 minutes, stirring occasionally.

RUNNING IRON ROAST

I heard a story one time about a feller that wanted to get in the cattle business so he went to the sale barn and inquired how this might be done. Much to his misfortune he fell prey to some local boys who sold him five choice breeding age steers and told him to take them home and just wait. Well, this feller was from the East and had formerly been an art teacher at some boarding school. He figured he could trust his new-found friends so he did. As luck would have it, on the way home he met a cowboy who said he would help this feller get his steers home for five dollars. Agreeing, this proud cattle owner told him his story. Well, the cowboy danged near fell off his horse laughing. The cowboy told him that steers don't breed, and that he had been cheated, but he told him they were right about one thing when they said to just wait—with his help he would have a nice cow herd in a few years.

Well, the cowboy was right. With the help of a fast horse, a sure rope, several moonlit nights and some artistic talent with a running iron, in three years the man from back East had five very fat steers and 100 head of the nicest breeding age heifers you could want.

a 4–5 lb. roast (any cut)
1 can cream of mushroom soup
1 package dehydrated onion soup mix

Spread onion soup mix in the bottom of a shallow baking pan, put the roast in on top. Pour the mushroom soup around. Cover this real tight with aluminum foil and bake for 3½ hours at 325 degrees.

4-F
('Cause it never was in the service)

When I cook I like to try things fixed a little different. When I was in the Marines they used to serve some stuff we called S.O.S. Ask anyone who was ever in the military to tell you what that means. It wasn't really that bad; we just had it an awful lot. The real name was creamed chipped beef and for years after my discharge from the service I couldn't even look at it until I learned this way of cooking it.

> 1 package chipped beef
> ½ cup finely chopped onion
> ½ cup milk
> 1 can cream of celery soup

Mix all this together in a skillet. Heat until good and hot, stirring occasionally. Serve over toast. Even an ex-Marine should like this.

Spur ranch, Texas—1910. *Cowboys around the Hoodlum wagon (wagon for hauling branding irons, tent poles, wood and other supplies).*

TODAY'S WRECK

When I worked for the G-Bar Ranch, we did all of our branding the old fashion way. You know, we had fun doing it and there wasn't any machinery to break down or alley ways for the critters to turn around in. We just took turns roping them and dragging 'em to the fire. Well, it was getting late in the season and we had already branded a couple thousand head and maybe we were getting tired and not alert like we should have been. Things started going from bad to worse.

The cattle wouldn't bunch, the calves wouldn't sort, we had a couple of break outs, and just all kinds of amazing things like that! After awhile things seemed to start going okay so we settled into our routine of branding. Picture if you will a big catch pen full of 300 calves, three cowboys riding horses, each with a calf roped sitting in the gate of this pen waiting for six cowboys mugging calves (that is two cowboys holding a calf down waiting for the iron). So now we have three calves being held by six cowboys in front of the gate, one running the hot iron branding each calf and two women are giving shots and one is keeping records and one ranch foreman making sure it all gets done. Just as we thought things were going smoothly, all hell broke loose! The calf on the left side of the gate decided he had been roped long enough and decided to try and get free so he ran under the belly of the middle horse and got him to bucking. I heard somebody yell "wreck" and looked up just in time to see two bucking horses being chased by two roped calves and two flying cowboys coming at us!

You would have thought somebody yelled "raid" at a brothel the way everybody was scattering. My lightning-quick brain told me to stay low, especially after one of them horses had freight-trained me and stepped on my elbow. The way the dust was flying an older man would have had flashbacks of the Dust Bowl. When everything settled we finally started laughing because no one was killed. Cowboys are like that—there might

OR Ranch, Arizona. 1909–1910. *The OR chuck wagon in a tight place.*

be a hell of a wreck but if nobody gets killed or hurt badly, it's instantly very funny.

We started estimating damages. One of the boys mugging got stepped on by his father's horse and got his leg broke, one of the boys that got bucked off landed on a needle full of combiotic (antibiotic) which he was allergic to, and I got the end of my elbow broke. Five horses out of eight spooked and broke their reins and ran off, and two of them still had calves tied to 'em. One of the horses kicked out a headlight on a truck, the ranch foreman got run over by damn near everything and all the boys mugging got run over by something. The feller running the branding iron threw it so it wouldn't burn anyone and it started a small grass fire. When we got everything caught, and got people ready to be hauled to the hospital, those of us who could stand were in a bunch laughing when the foreman got that big ol smile on his face and said, "Damn, ain't this fun?"

Believe it or not, this inspired another name for a mess I like to cook up every so often. Later the same day a couple of the fellers came home with me for supper and while I was fixing it one of the guys asked what it was and I told him I didn't know and he allowed as how it was all mixed up, it reminded him of the day's wreck and from that day on it became known as "Today's Wreck."

In about 3 tablespoons shortening (don't use lard) sauté:

> 1 green pepper, diced
> 2 large onions, sliced
> 1 lb. ground beef—when beef is browned, add:
>
> 2½ cups cooked tomatoes
> 1½ teaspoons chili powder
> ⅔ cup uncooked rice
> salt & pepper to taste

Mix this all up in a large skillet, cover, and cook for about one hour over low heat. This ain't bad, especially with fry bread! (Saddlebag bread)

T. L.'s Traveling Tid Bits for Two
or
Foil Cooking on the Freeway

Back when I was going down the road with visions of being a world champion bull rider, which I never was, we used to travel in a bunch of five or six guys all sharing the cost of our ventures equally. If we were lucky in the draw and three or four of us got our stock covered and made it to the pay window, it was party time, good restaurants, booze, and a danged good time! Much like the fabled grasshopper, to heck with tomorrow, let's have a good time tonight! Also, as in the grasshopper and ant fable, when the party was over, we were broke and it was grasshopper winter again! With only enough money to pay entry fees and buy gas, we'd head down the road toward the next rodeo. When there wasn't enough money in the "kitty" for a fast food delight we soon learned to cook from scratch. I don't mean start with all the basics and create a culinary delight. I mean where you scratch your head and wonder how the hell you're going to feed six hungry cowboys with only six dollars, and the next problem, how are you going to cook it while traveling?

Cowboys are natural born problem makers and solvers, so this was no big deal. We would buy hamburger, or hot dogs, a bunch of carrots, a small bag of spuds, salt and pepper, a loaf of bread, and a roll of aluminum foil. With all these ingredients we gave a new meaning to fast food!

> 1 lb. ground beef
> 2 carrots (medium sized)
> 3 potatoes (not too small)
> salt & pepper to taste
> water, if available (or anything drinkable that won't burn)
> 1 tablespoon margarine (if you have it)

Shape four standard burgers from ground beef, salt and pepper to taste. Lay burgers side by side—two per package—on sheets of foil big enough to fold and seal burgers in a tight packet. Always remember to have all folds and seams tight as not to let natural juices leak. Slice carrots so they are round, not long, about ¼ inch thick. Clean potatoes but don't peel them, cut in chunks. Then salt and pepper to your liking. Tear off a big enough sheet of aluminum foil to wrap the vegetables in and place them on the foil, pull up ends to form a makeshift pan. Add a little water, put in your margarine, and seal like you did the burgers. Place in a cool place in your car or truck and start driving for about fifteen minutes or until your engine is good and hot. Pull off the highway to a safe place, raise your hood and place the three foil packets on the manifold each in its own place with one side touching a hot part of the engine. After you close the hood (once closed, the food packets should not foul engine parts—fan belts, spark plugs & etc.), start driving again.

In the old days of big engines and 70 miles per hour speed limits, in about one half hour you would stop and turn 'em over and cook for another one half hour, pull into a road side park or gas station, remove the packets and enjoy the real meaning of fast food!

A few words of caution are in order. Now that EPA, OSHA, and every other letter of the alphabet have formed groups to tell us what we can and cannot do with our own lives, I can't be sure the above times will work on all cars or trucks. You will just have to experiment until things are cooked to your liking. Cooking at 70 mph and on a 409 cubic inch engine, I could just about tell you when the meat was rare, medium or well done. Sometimes you needed to cook your vegetables for 37 miles before adding the burgers, but with today's smaller engines and 55 mph speed limit I can't be sure.

P.S. If you drive a compact car and pull into a service station before you're done cooking, don't forget to remind the attendant that the big aluminum thing is your lunch and the small aluminum thing is your engine! I don't think a quart of 10/W40 in your carrots would be very good.

LS Ranch, Texas. 1908. *The LS outfit at the chuckwagon having dinner in the shade of a tree.*

SHEEP IN THE GARDEN

Now I want to tell you I'm a cow man at heart, always have been, always will be. A friend of mine who raises woolies (sheep to most people) flat gave me hell for not having any mention of how to cook lamb or mutton or stuff like that. I realized there might be others out there who enjoy a rack of lamb or lamb chops or some other cut of the critter, so I did some digging and asked a few sheep herders for ways to cook it. I thought maybe I just hadn't learned how to cook it correctly and maybe that was why I didn't like it. Well, I was wrong, I don't like it any way you cook it! But for those of you who do, here are some good recipes tested and approved by a sheep herder friend of mine.

3 lbs. boneless lamb (front quarter cut will be fine)

⅓ cup finely chopped carrots

2 tablespoons chopped parsley

2 tablespoons finely chopped onion

flour

salt & pepper to taste

2½ tablespoons bacon drippings

2–4 tablespoons cornstarch

Cut lamb into bite size pieces, roll in flour, and brown in the bacon drippings. Season the flour with salt and pepper if you want to. Put browned lamb in the bottom of a casserole dish and add all the other ingredients. Cover with water and cook in the oven until the meat is tender. It should take about 1½ hours at 350 degrees. Season to taste and thicken gravy with cornstarch. (Mix 2–4 tablespoons of cornstarch with small amount of cool water and gradually add to the juices to thicken for gravy.)

SLEEPIN' SHEEP

This one actually wasn't really too bad as far as lamb goes. I thought that the way this is fixed and the fact that you have to wait overnight to fix it made it deserving of the name "Sleepin' Sheep."

2½ lbs. boneless lamb
2 tablespoons onions, minced
2 tablespoons parsley, minced
4 tablespoons vinegar
3 tablespoons cooking oil

Cut meat into strips and thump 'em with a tenderizer hammer. Mix all the seasonings and oil and vinegar together, pour over the meat, and let stand overnight. When you're ready to cook it, put it in a hot pan and sauté until well cooked and tender.

LAMB CHOPS

Another good friend of mine gave me this recipe for fixing lamb chops. He said it was his favorite.

Take some lamb chops, place each on an oak board cut just larger than the chops, put them in the bottom of a deep covered pan. On top, place: celery, carrots, potatoes, cut into stew size bits, salt, pepper, a little garlic salt, and 6 cups strong beef broth. Cover pan with a lid and bake in the oven until everything is done and tender. Remove from oven and place the vegetables in a dish, put the boards on a meat platter, throw the chops away and hope they didn't mess up that good beef broth or vegetables!

Now I haven't said too many really nice things about sheep and I hope I haven't made too many people mad. All the people I know who raise sheep are truly nice, kind, wonderful folks. I don't care if the smell does spook my horse when they stop by for a visit!

Three Block Ranch, near Richardson, New Mexico. 1905–1910. *Some Block cowboys helping the wagon cook pitch camp on the range of the El Capitan Land and Cattle Company.*

POULTRY AND FOWL

ひ귀 NX ┴ ⊙ # ⊛ ∞ ox ∾ ᴗᴣ

ROASTED DUCK

It gets pretty tough sometimes to concentrate on everyday problems when you've met as many wonderful people as I have. People try to tell me that one part of our country is nicer than others. Well, I've met really nice folks everywhere. I believe that folks are basically kind and thoughtful and it's just that you hear only about the bad things people do. I think one day a week the dadgum news media should set aside an hour to tell about the good things people do. Well, enough of my soap-box preaching and back to this story. Some of the fine folks I've met live in Lakeland, Florida.

I was in their fair city late in the fall of the year and duck season was just opening and one of them inquired if I would like to go waste a box of shells shooting holes in the sky—he knew we couldn't hit any ducks. I told him I would like to but I didn't have a license or shotgun. The license was no problem, as we would be hunting with a game warden and he would sell me one. As far as a shotgun was concerned, my friend said I could use his since he had just that morning bought a brand new one just for duck hunting. When I asked if each man had enough life insurance, I think for a little bit they were wishing they hadn't asked me to go, but one of the fellers had seen me shoot before and assured the others I was only joking. We had a little laugh and I told them I'd love to go.

Later that night we loaded all our stuff into a van and headed for eastern Florida for some good times. Upon reaching our destination we had a quick breakfast and off to the boats we went. When we paired up, my friend and I ended up in one boat while the others went to the blinds and another boat. Well, as we went out towards some marshy shores we quietly talked about days past and days to come, and had an all around pleasant conversation, realizing the true meaning of friendship. Then we settled in for some shooting.

We had a few minutes before daylight and I figured since I had never done any shooting with this gun I'd better look it over and figure out how it worked. This finally done, I loaded and sat and waited while my friend did the same. He had just taken his out of the new box when we'd left the van and he was really giving it the once over.

I don't know if it was the conversation over the new gun or the excitement of the hunt, but all of a sudden it was daybreak and we could hear the boys in the other boat start with their calls and we heard the real ducks answer. My friend loads his gun and we get ready for the shootin' to start! Well, here they came, a big bunch of them and they were flying low enough to shoot, so shoot we did, one shot each. I got lucky and scored a hit. He got unlucky and his brand new shotgun blew up! It scared the hell out of both of us! I remember little particles of stuff and a big chuck of something hitting me up side the head, him grabbing his head and dropping that gun. I thought the world had come to an end! After the dust settled, we looked at each other, saw neither of us was hurt bad and in unison we asked "What the hell happened?" We found the whole side of his shotgun blown away, and being quick to reason, we figured out where the shower of debris came from. After a few more obscenities, the laughter started between us. It just seemed like the thing to do especially since I had made a point of asking if their life insurance was paid and I didn't have a dime's worth on me. I didn't think I would need it.

While duck hunting, I got lucky twice, once by not getting killed or hurt when the gun blew up and once when I learned a really good way to cook duck.

1 duck (cleaned and dry)
flour
wild rice
salt & pepper to taste
3–4 strips bacon
¼ large onion, chopped
1 cup chicken bouillon
water

Sprinkle flour generously on duck, salt and pepper, put duck aside for awhile. Prepare enough wild rice to stuff the duck. Season with salt and pepper and onion. Fasten each piece of bacon across the duck with toothpicks. Stuff the duck with rice and place in a roaster. Cover the bottom of the roaster with the bouillon and water. Cover tightly and cook at 350 degrees in the oven for 2 hours or until the duck is done. Be sure to baste it ever so often with the natural juices collecting in the pan and remove the cover for the last fifteen minutes so the skin can cook to a golden brown.

Shoe Bar Ranch, Texas. 1901–1910. *Some of the Shoe Bar cowboys having dinner at the chuck wagon.*

L S range, Lincoln County, near Tascosa, New Mexico. 1907–1910 (?) *Five L S cowpunchers sitting beside the chuck wagon for a mid-day rest.*

LUCKY SHOT

Being from Iowa, I'm fortunate to get to go pheasant hunting in one of the best regions in the country. Rooster pheasants are plentiful in my territory and ever once in a while one will commit suicide and fly into one of my shots. I figure it must be self-inflicted 'cause I ain't that good a shot. This is the way I really like to cook 'em.

1 pheasant
bacon
salt & pepper
1 cup chicken bouillon
butter, melted
flour

Cover pheasant (of course it's cleaned and soaked) with bacon. Use a string to keep the bacon in place or try toothpicks. Put the bird in a roasting pan and pour enough water and bouillon over the bird to allow for self basting. Roast for 20 to 30 minutes at 375–400 degrees, depending on the size of the bird. Remove the bacon and brush on the melted butter, sprinkle with flour, and put it back in the oven until it is a golden brown.

Shoe Bar Ranch, Texas. 1905–1910. *Shoe Bar boys having dinner at the chuck wagon; sitting on bedrolls.*

SOUTHERN HOSPITALITY
(Cornish Game Hen)

On one of my many travels I met a feller in Louisiana who had considerable money. Along with his money he also owned several thousand acres, a cotton gin, a lumber company, one hell of a mansion, and a summer house almost as big. This guy had a fine collection of some really good horses and owned some of the best in the country.

One day while we were out at the summer house riding some cutting horses, one of the servants came out to the arena to inform us that lunch was ready. I want to tell you this little lunch was quite a spread. There was stuff I don't even know today what it was! The one thing that stuck in my mind was the way they had prepared the quail. Now those quail were some of the best I've ever eaten. Since then I've tried cooking cornish game hens the same way and they turn out almost as good.

½ cornish game hen for each person
salt & pepper
flour

Roll each half of bird in flour, salt and pepper to taste. Fill deep fat fryer half full of hot fat. Drop in the birds and cook for a few minutes on hot, then reduce the heat and cover fryer. Cook until tender, and be sure to turn the birds to the other side when golden brown—not dark. You can serve these with anything. Some of that chicken flavored rice they have on the market is danged good!

GOT-TO-GO POT PIE

The story goes that once upon a time this big lousy, mean, burly, ornery, nasty, vicious, terrible (and those are his good points) feller rides into this town and he was riding a grizzly bear using a barbed wire bit to guide him and a six foot rattlesnake as a whip to keep the bear going! Seems this feller stopped at the only saloon in town, ran inside and bellered at the bartender to give him a keg of beer and to make it quick. The bartender, seeing the likes of this feller, did just that. When the stranger finished, the bartender asked if he would like another. The feller just wiped his mouth with his sleeve and said "Hell no, I ain't got time, I've got to get out of here before that mean son-of-a-bitch chasing me catches up!"

Now I never met the feller but I'll bet even he would have time to fix this.

    1 can boned chicken (6 oz.)
    1 package frozen mixed vegetables, thawed
    ⅓ cup water
    1 can cream of chicken soup
    1 can biscuits

Mix everything in a pan. Heat and bring to a boil until the vegetables are done. Pour into a casserole dish and place biscuits on top of it. Put it in the oven and bake until the biscuits are done, at the temperature recommended on the can of biscuits.

MOMMA'S SUNDAY FRIED CHICKEN

3–4 lb. cut up fryer (the smaller the pieces the better)
2½ cups flour
½ cup yellow cornmeal
1 teaspoon salt to start (add more according to your taste)
¼ teaspoon pepper to start (add more according to your taste)
1 egg
1½ cups milk

Soak fryer in salt water for at least ½ hour. Mix flour, cornmeal, salt and pepper. In separate bowl mix milk and egg. Dip chicken in milk mixture until well soaked and then dip in flour mixture until well coated. Drop into hot vegetable oil deep enough to cover half or more of chicken pieces. Brown on one side to golden brown before turning. When golden brown on both sides, remove and drain. Don't cook too fast—usually a medium high heat—and don't let the cowgirl or cowboy in the room distract you from watching your chicken so it gets just the right shade of brown, fit for a king and not a burnt offering to the gods!

This chicken will make you lick your fingers twice and scrape the dish for more crispies!

WAGON SEAT SURPRISE

On the trail the cook used to sit on the chuck wagon seat and shoot prairie chickens, pheasants, or grouse and fixed these things for the men (if he was in a good mood, which wasn't often). The surprise came when the men bit into these because they didn't know what would be inside.

1 can biscuits (refrigerator type, unless you want to make your own)
½ cup of your favorite cheese, diced
2 tablespoons mayonnaise
¼ cup chicken, cooked and diced (pheasant, grouse, quail, or any bird you want)
1 tablespoon melted butter
¼ cup diced celery

Flatten each biscuit into a thin oval, put half of them on a greased cookie sheet or shallow cake pan. Mix everything except the melted butter and spoon over the biscuits. Place remaining biscuits on top of the mixture and press the edges together. Brush the melted butter on top and bake in preheated oven at 425 degrees for 15 minutes.

If you ain't in a good mood when you cook these, you will be when you eat 'em.

CHICKEN LIVERS À LA GOOD!

1 lb. bacon
1 lb. chicken livers (washed thoroughly)
2 cups flour
¾ teaspoon salt
¼ teaspoon pepper
1 egg, beaten
½ cup milk
vegetable oil
toothpicks

Mix flour, salt, pepper. Mix beaten egg and milk. Dip each liver in milk and egg mixture, then in flour mixture until thoroughly covered. Roll liver in a strip of bacon and fasten with a toothpick. Small pieces may need only ½ piece of bacon. Drop in medium hot vegetable oil, deep enough to cover at least half of each liver. Cook on medium to medium high heat until all sides are a golden brown. Be careful not to overcook so liver won't be hard. Remove and drain. Then serve and watch them disappear. Even a chronic liver hater will love them!

Matador Ranch, Texas. 1908. *A Matador cowboy leading the way for the chuck wagon driver while moving the outfit.*

CHICKEN AND DUMPLINGS

CHICKEN:

1 3–4 lb. chicken boiled in about 3 qts. water

3–4 chicken bouillon cubes

¼ teaspoon onion powder

3 celery stalks diced

½ stick butter or margarine

Boil all this slowly in a heavy covered dutch oven or large heavy kettle until the chicken begins to fall away from the bones. Remove the chicken. Slice to serve on a platter or remove it from the bones and return to the kettle. To this, add the dumplings.

DUMPLINGS:

4 cups flour

8 teaspoons baking powder

½ teaspoon pepper

2 teaspoons salt

2 large eggs, well beaten

6 tablespoons melted butter

1⅓ cups milk

Sift all dry ingredients together. Make a well in the middle of the mixture and pour in the eggs, butter, and milk. It should make a stiff batter. Drop by teaspoonfuls in the boiling broth by dipping the spoon in and letting the broth remove the batter from the spoon. Do not stir but cover the kettle tightly and simmer for about 15 to 20 minutes. Dumplings will be biscuit-like inside.

Serve these with the chicken and a vegetable or salad. You'll fill at least 4–6 hungry cowboys and they'll be begging for invitations back!!

Spur Ranch, Texas—1907. *A few of the Spur cowboys taking it easy around the chuckwagon.*

PORK

ꝲ ꝲ ꝲ ꝲ ꝲ ꝲ ꝲ ꝲ ꝲ ꝲ ꝲ ꝲ ꝲ ꝲ ꝲ

DEVIL HOG

My old man sure did like to eat. He would eat just about anything. If you could cook it he'd try it. Well, one of his favorites was ham fixed just about any way you could fix it. Being as how Dad was a preacher, I like to call this one "Devil Hog" because it tastes so good it's got to be evil!

        3 lbs. thick sliced ham
        1 cup brown sugar
        10 slices pineapple
        6 or 7 sweet potatoes, peeled

Brown ham on one side, then place it brown side up in a big dutch oven or covered baking dish large enough to handle it. Put potatoes around the ham and sprinkle everything with brown sugar. Cook for 1 hour and 10 minutes. Then turn the meat, and put pineapple slices on top and pour the juice over everything. Roll the potatoes around in that juice and cook for another 30 minutes.

AW BOLOGNA

Sometimes things can get pretty ho-hum around a feller's house and even the little punchers are eager for something different. Well, don't despair, there is a way to make them happy even on a tight budget.

bologna
mashed potatoes (last night's leftovers would be great)
cheese slices

Brown the bologna on both sides, then put the slices on a cookie sheet. Scoop an ice cream dipper of mashed potatoes on each piece and top with a cheese slice. Bake until cheese melts.

Serve this with a can of pork'n'beans and watch the smiles show up on them little punchers.

HOG

I can't really remember where this came from but I know they sure are good when you need something to munch on while watching a rodeo or a ball game on TV, or if you're oiling your saddle or mending tack or just anything. I just call 'em "Hog."

    2 lbs. sausage
    1½ cups milk
    2 cups grated cheese (cheddar is good)
    5 cups dry biscuit mix

Mix everything together and roll into small balls. Put on an ungreased pizza pan, cookie sheet, or any similar pan, and bake for 25 minutes at 350 degrees.

Matador Ranch, Texas. 1908. *Matador chuck wagon crossing sandy bottom of a dry river.*

SIDE DISHES

JА Рᒪ NX ᒀ ᐤ # Ⓐ ᗤ ox ⌐ 凸 入

AUNT GEORGE'S SWEET POTATOES
(Her name wasn't really George, we just called her that)

Now I want to tell you that sweet potatoes used to be one of my family favorites, along with macaroni and cheese. We had sweet spuds fixed just about any way you could think of, but this was the way one of my late aunts used to fix 'em and they sure are danged good this way!

3 cups mashed, cooked, sweet potatoes
3 tablespoons butter (don't use margarine unless you have to)
½ teaspoon salt
¼ teaspoon paprika (looks nice and gives a little flavor)
2 egg yolks
2 egg whites, beaten stiff
½ cup diced pineapple (use a little bit of the juice—not much)

Mix potatoes, butter, salt, paprika, and yolks. Beat two minutes. Fold in beaten egg whites and pineapple. Spread in buttered baking dish—you don't have to be real neat. Bake in moderate oven for 15 minutes. Serve 'em right from the baking dish.

NOODLES

4 cups flour
2–3 eggs, well beaten
1 teaspoon salt
¼ teaspoon pepper
chicken broth or water
3–4 drops yellow food coloring

Put flour, salt, and pepper in a large bowl. Add well-beaten eggs, food color, and enough broth or water to make a dough. Roll out on floured board or pastry sheet to about ⅛ inch thickness. Cut into size of noodles desired (large or small, wide or narrow) using a pastry wheel or steak knife.

If you have time, let the noodles dry out for an hour or so before dropping into the prepared chicken broth. Cover and simmer 15 to 20 minutes, or until the noodles are tender.

CORN CAKES

2 eggs, beaten
1 teaspoon salt
1 teaspoon sugar
3 cups buttermilk
1 teaspoon soda, dissolved in a little hot water
corn meal

Mix all this together and add enough meal to make a thin batter. Cook on a slightly greased griddle like pancakes until golden brown. Goes good with Enchilada Filling.

ENCHILADA FILLING

1 cup chopped onions
½ cup longhorn cheese (grated)
2 eggs
6 strips bacon
1 teaspoon chili powder
2 cans whole tomatoes

Cut up bacon strips and fry crisp. Add half of the chopped onions, cook until tender. Add chili powder and tomatoes. Let simmer for at least an hour. Scramble eggs in separate skillet. Place in corn cakes and sprinkle in rest of chopped onions and grated cheese and pour sauce over each cake.

I like this with a little Tabasco sauce on mine!

HOT & SPICY REFRIED BEANS

1 16 oz. can refried beans
2 slices bacon
1½ teaspoons chili powder
¼ cup shredded jack cheese
1 tomato, diced
lettuce leaves

Cook bacon in skillet until crisp. Remove; drain on paper towels; crumble. Add chili powder to fat left in skillet. Cook, stirring constantly, 1 minute. Stir in refried beans and bacon and heat until thoroughly hot all the way through—using low heat and stirring constantly. Remove from heat and place a generous amount on lettuce leaves spread on salad plate. Top with shredded jack cheese and diced tomatoes. Delicious served with garlic bread or taco chips. Makes 2–4 servings.

Now if this ain't hot enough for you—I like mine a little hotter—add a few peppers or a little Tabasco sauce!

VEGETABLE CASSEROLE

1 package frozen brussels sprouts
1 package frozen broccoli pieces (or fresh vegetables)
1 package frozen cauliflower (or fresh)
2 cans cream of mushroom soup
1–2 cans milk (enough to just about cover the vegetables)
¼ teaspoon garlic powder or salt
1 cup bread crumbs
cheddar cheese
4 tablespoons butter

Place the vegetables, soup, milk and salt in large casserole dish and mix. Slice cheese in thin strips and place along entire top of the casserole. On top of the cheese, sprinkle the bread crumbs, and then dot the butter over the crumbs.

Place in 350 degree oven and bake until tender and bread crumbs are a golden brown (about 45 minutes to an hour).

This is also great with sliced potatoes or green beans. If you're in a hurry, omit the bread crumbs and simmer all in a covered dish on top of the stove or in your microwave.

LS Ranch, Texas. 1908. *An LS cook mixing dough at the business end of a chuckwagon.*

BREADS, ETC.

ᴊᴧ ꝵ ɴx ⅃ ⊙ # Ⓐ ∽ ox ⌁ ⊡ ⱌ

GOOD STUFF

I learned this one from a cowboy friend of mine that was working in a feedlot in Oklahoma and he learned it from his mother. He didn't know what she called it so we just called it "Good Stuff."

     1 cup flour
     1 qt. milk
     salt & pepper
     2 tablespoons butter (margarine if you have to)
     water

Put the flour in a bowl. Form little dough balls of various sizes by dropping a few drops of water at a time in the flour and stirring gently. Do this until you have about 1½ cups dough balls made. Heat the milk in a sauce pan on medium heat and add butter, salt, and pepper to taste. When this mixture just starts to boil add the dough balls and bring milk just to the boiling stage again. Take off the stove and serve.

When your stomach gets to yelling for something good and quick, go out to the kitchen and whip up some of that "Good Stuff."

Spur Ranch, Texas. 1907. *The Spur outfit is entertaining a gentleman and a lady at the noonday meal. An unusually elaborate spread to have a table as well as a tent.*

BISCUITS

5 cups all purpose flour
¾ cup vegetable shortening
      Mix together until you have a crumbly mixture.
1 teaspoon soda
3 tablespoons sugar (may mix with dissolving yeast to help it grow faster)
3 teaspoons baking powder
2 cups buttermilk
1 yeast cake dissolved in ½ cup water

Add rest of dry ingredients to crumbly mixture. Add buttermilk and dissolved yeast. Work together with a large spoon until all flour is moistened. Cover bowl and put in refrigerator.

When ready to use, take out as much as is needed, roll on floured board to ½ inch thickness and cut. Bake at 400 degrees on a cookie sheet or in a shallow pan about 12 minutes or until lightly browned. Makes about five dozen light, flaky biscuits. Pan should be lightly greased.

This dough will keep for several weeks in the refrigerator. It also makes very good doughnuts, topping for a main dish, or you can let it rise as rolls.

O R range, Arizona—1910. *One of the O R cowpunchers watching the cook tend the fire after a noon meal at the wagon.*

SADDLEBAG BREAD
(Indian Fry Bread)

4 cups sifted flour
1½ cups lukewarm milk
¼ cup warm water
1 cake or 1 package yeast
1 tablespoon sugar
1 tablespoon shortening
1 teaspoon baking powder
1½ teaspoons salt

Heat shortening in a big heavy pan or dutch oven, deep enough to cook several of these things at a time (about 4 to 6 inches deep). Dissolve yeast in warm water with sugar and add to milk. Combine dry ingredients and cut in shortening until crumbly. Add liquid to flour mixture and mix well, then knead about 5 to 10 minutes. Roll dough out to about ¼ inch thickness, pinch off pieces and shape into balls. Roll each ball out thin, cut through the middle, and drop into hot shortening, turning once. When light golden brown, remove and drain on paper towel.

To use this as a dessert, roll in powdered sugar when just removed from hot shortening—may be served with fresh honey.

These are fantastic stuffed with chili or Hot & Spicy Refried Beans, or just as a snack to satisfy that ever-present craving for something good and different!

Matador Ranch, Texas. 1906. *The Matador Wagon Cook making a cobbler.*

SWETS

MOMMA'S FRITTERS

I want to tell you that cowboys ain't all horse sweat and wang leather, we like a few nice things and some of the niceties in life we like are sweets—pies, cakes, doughnuts, candy, etc. I remember my mom used to make some little things she called fritters. They were sure good on a cold night with hot chocolate!

    1 cup flour
    2 eggs, well beaten
    ½ teaspoon salt
    ⅔ cup milk

Mix the milk and eggs together. Slowly add them to the flour and salt which you've already mixed together. This will make a thick batter. Drop by spoonfuls into hot fat, heated to about 380 degrees. Fry on both sides until brown—about 1½ minutes each side. Remove from fat, drain on paper towels. Roll in powdered sugar and have the hot chocolate ready!

LS Ranch, Texas. 1908. *Cowboys pulling the LS chuckwagon over a bad place as the outfit trails out of a canyon.*

MOLASSES CUSTARD PIE

Before everything was deep fat fried, and Fast Food Freddies started cooking in all the restaurants, the best meals you could get while traveling were at truck stops. At one of my many 2:00 a.m. stops for coffee, gas, rest, and pie, I had the honor of meeting the pie baker at a little truck stop in Nebraska and she had just finished cooling her fresh baked custard pies. After a little persuasion she finally gave me her recipe.

1 cup sugar
2 tablespoons butter (the real stuff)
1½ cup molasses
4 eggs (yolks & whites separated & beaten)

Cream butter and sugar, add to beaten egg yolks. Add molasses and mix well. Fold in stiffly beaten egg whites. Pour all this into an unbaked crust and bake at 350 degrees until a knife comes out clean when stuck in the middle.

When I eat this, I think of the days when the word "food" flashing in the night meant *good*, not fast fixed, fast frozen, fast fried, and fast forgotten!

COWBOY'S CANDY BAR

4 cups oatmeal

1 cup margarine

½ cup white corn syrup

1 cup brown sugar

6 oz. package chocolate chips

¾ cup crunchy peanut butter

Mix oatmeal, margarine, corn syrup, and sugar as for a pie crust. Pat in bottom of a greased 9 × 13 inch pan. Bake at 350 degrees for 10–15 minutes. Cool. Melt a 6 ounce package of chocolate chips and add to ¾ cup chunky peanut butter. Spread over baked layer. Refrigerate. Cut into squares before completely hardened.

Matador Ranch, Texas. 1908. *The Matador chuck wagon on the move, followed by the hoodlum wagon.*

ANGUS CAKES

Preheat oven to 350 degrees, grease and flour 8 × 8 glass baking dish.

Sift together: ¾ cup flour
             ½ teaspoon baking powder
             ¼ teaspoon salt
             6 tablespoons cocoa
Melt ½ cup shortening, let cool, then mix in:
1 cup sugar
2 eggs
½ teaspoon vanilla
flour mixture
½ cup nuts if desired

Spread batter in greased dish and bake on rack slightly below the center of the oven for 25 minutes. Do not over-bake! They should be soft and chewy.

Matador Ranch, Texas. 1891. *Photograph of the Matador outfit eating at the chuck wagon at the time Murdo Mackenzie (center, with black hat and beard) took over the management of the ranch. At the extreme right is H. H. ("Paint") Campbell who established the ranch in 1879 with a half-dugout for headquarters.*

TEXAS PECAN CAKE

1¼ cup butter
1½ cup sugar
4 unbeaten eggs
3 cups flour
2 teaspoons baking powder
½ teaspoon salt
2 teaspoons vanilla
1 cup milk
2 cups chopped pecans

Prepare:
   Toast nuts in ¼ cup butter in 350 degree oven for 20–25 minutes—stirring often. Cream butter (1 cup) and sugar until smooth. Beat in eggs one at a time. Sift together flour, salt, and baking powder, then add alternately with milk. Stir in vanilla and 1⅓ cups pecans. Bake in three 8 inch layer pans which are greased and floured—in 350 degree oven for 25–30 minutes. Cool, then frost (No, I didn't forget the rest of the nuts, and I didn't eat them. Read on.)

FROSTING

Cream ½ cup margarine and ½ cup vegetable shortening. Add 1 pound powdered sugar and ½ teaspoon vanilla. Add milk a tablespoon at a time until you have a smooth creamy mixture. *Add remaining pecans*. Spread between each layer and on top of Texas Pecan Cake.

O R range, Arizona. 1910. *A day herder of the O R having a bite to eat at the chuck wagon.*

MY OWN WESTERN PECAN PIE

4 cups peeled and sliced apples
½ cup maple syrup
1 teaspoon vanilla
½ cup sugar
½ teaspoon cinnamon
2 teaspoons cornstarch
½ cup water
2 tablespoons butter or margarine
½ cup pecans, broken into pieces

Toss apple slices with mixture of sugar, cinnamon, vanilla until thoroughly coated. Place in 9 inch pan lined with unbaked pie shell. Mix cornstarch and water and drizzle over apples. Pour syrup over top of all. Sprinkle nuts over all. Top with lattice crust and dot margarine over openings. Bake at 375 degrees for 45–60 minutes until filling is bubbly and crust is light golden brown.

CRUST

1¼ cup lard
3 cups flour
1 beaten egg
5 tablespoons water
1 teaspoon vinegar
1 teaspoon salt

Cut lard into flour mixture until crumbly. Add vinegar and small amounts of water and mix until of kneading consistency. Roll out on floured board and line pie pans. Makes enough for three 9 inch pies.

Matador Ranch, Spur, Texas. 1908. *The Matador wagon cook, Harry Stewart, making a cobbler.*

CATTLE KATE'S CAKE

In large mixing bowl mix:

> 2 cups flour
>
> 2 cups sugar

In heavy pan, bring to boil:

> ½ cup vegetable shortening
>
> 1 stick margarine
>
> 1 cup water
>
> 4 tablespoons cocoa

Cool slightly

Pour over flour and sugar and add:

> ½ cup milk
>
> 1 teaspoon vanilla
>
> 1 teaspoon soda
>
> 1 teaspoon cinnamon (optional)
>
> 2 eggs

Blend well. Grease and flour cookie sheet or large sheet cake pan. Pour in mix and bake at 350 degrees for 20 minutes. While cake is baking, prepare icing.

ICING

> 1 stick butter or margarine
>
> ¼ cup white corn syrup
>
> 4 tablespoons cocoa
>
> 6 tablespoons milk
>
> 1 lb. box powdered sugar

Bring first four ingredients to boil. Add powdered sugar. Mix thoroughly and pour over cake while warm. It should spread by itself and be a creamy glaze.

LS Ranch, Texas. 1908. *The LS outfit trailing out of a canyon while the cowboys help pull the chuckwagon over a bad place.*

WHO THE HELL KNOWS

As I travel across this country I'm very often asked to join folks for a home cooked meal, which I very rarely turn down because I feel any home cooked meal has got to be good. I might add I've never been disappointed, even the bad ones serve as a *good* example of what a bad meal really is. Now when these offers are extended I start wondering—do I look so pale they think I ain't eating right; or is it I'm so danged big they figure I'll eat anything? Whatever the case, I'm always ready to put the feed bag on!

One time in Texas this fine family asked me to a dinner of fried chicken with all the trimmings. Being a full time lover of crisp, crunchy fried chicken, I was in their car before they could change their minds, then I said, "Yes, I'd love to." Little did I know that before dinner was done we would have time to ride three colts that somehow had managed to reach the age of four without being touched. The family figured this would be a good time to do as the phone company says and "reach out and touch 'em." Well, I don't know who was touching who the most but by the time dinner was ready I was wishing I had never heard of a chicken. But for the grace of the Almighty and my incurable desire for fried chicken we got them broncs to where they finally agreed to a truce and let us get away with only cuts, bruises and a couple of broken fingers, not to mention the teeth marks when them horses tried to have us for dinner.

After tending our wounds we all sat down to one of the best home cooked meals I have ever had the pleasure of eating! We had crisp, crunchy fried chicken, creamy smooth mashed potatoes with just enough lumps in 'em to let you know they weren't instant, milk gravy fixed in the skillet with the crunchies from the chicken, home grown green beans and home canned tomatoes and homemade bread. Boy, I thought there was no topping what I was eating. But then it happened. I realized this sweet family must've been trying to kill me! First them broncs, then that fine, fine meal and now . . . dessert.

That lady brought out a bowl of stuff that was out of this world! When I asked what it was, the man of the house said, "Who the hell knows?" I thought he was pulling my leg but when he asked his wife for the real name, her answer was the same. It seems some-one had copied the recipe from a book or newspaper and didn't write down the name. From that day on, it was given the name "Who The Hell Knows."

1 cup sugar
½ cup flour
⅓ teaspoon salt
2 cups evaporated milk
4 tablespoons margarine, plus a couple drops of yellow food color for a rich look
3 eggs, separated
1 teaspoon vanilla

Mix flour, salt, and sugar in a pan. Beat egg yolks and milk together till smooth and add to above. Add butter. Cook and stir rapidly until it all thickens. Let cool and add vanilla. Beat egg whites until stiff, add ¼ cup sugar and mix thoroughly. Put this all in a pyrex bowl and top with the meringue. In a separate dish place a serving of this dessert suitable to your liking, cause when this hits the dining table, there might not be enough left for you!

"RED HOT" APPLES

4–6 medium to large apples, peeled & sliced
2–3 tablespoons butter
½ cup sugar
½ bag "Red Hot" candies

Place apples in a heavy fry pan with the butter and sugar. Cover tightly and simmer slowly until the apples are tender. Add the Red Hots and cover until they are melted and thoroughly mixed with the apples. The apples should still be firm, not mushy, and they should be red.

If more Red Hots are needed, add them and serve warm. These are great morning noon and night and they warm you clear down to your boots! They're also great when you're out on the range, you run into an apple tree and just happen to have a fry pan with you with a little sugar and butter!

THANK YOU JOHNNY

2 cups peeled and diced apples
1 cup sugar
1 egg
1 cup sifted flour
1½ teaspoon cinnamon
1 teaspoon soda
½ cup chopped nuts

Mix sugar with apples and let stand until sugar is dissolved; add eggs, beat well. Sift dry ingredients together and stir into apple mixture, add nuts, pour into 8 inch pan. Bake at 375 degrees for 40 minutes or until top springs back when touched. Remove from oven and immediately cover with hot glaze. Say thank you to Johnny Appleseed for planting all them seeds and growing all them apples!!

HOT GLAZE

½ cup brown sugar
½ cup granulated sugar
2 tablespoons flour
1 cup water
¼ cup margarine
1 teaspoon vanilla
pinch of salt

Heat all to boiling stage. Turn to simmer and simmer slowly for 10 minutes. Pour over top of cake.

JA Ranch, Texas. 1907. *The JA chuckwagon camped on Cotton Wood Creek.*

BUFFALO CHIPS

1 yellow cake mix
2 eggs
1 cup peanut butter
½ cup melted margarine

Mix well and spread ⅔ cup of dough on a large cookie sheet. In sauce pan melt together:

2 tablespoons butter or margarine
1 12 ounce package chocolate chips
1 can sweetened condensed milk
½ teaspoon salt
2 teaspoons vanilla

Remove from heat—add 1 cup coconut (optional) and spread over dough. Drop remaining dough over top and sprinkle nuts over top of mixture. Bake at 350 degrees for 10–15 minutes. Cut into squares.

BETTER BY THE POUND

Cream: ½ lb. butter

½ cup soft shortening

Add: 3 cups sugar

5 eggs

1 teaspoon vanilla

Sift together and add alternately with milk:

3 cups flour

½ teaspoon baking powder

½ teaspoon salt

4 tablespoons cocoa

1 cup milk

Bake in tube pan in 325 degree oven for 1 hour and 10 minutes.

This is great served warm with soft butter spread on each piece. May be frosted if you desire.

When the day's work is done, dawn comes all too soon.

FRUIT SALAD

Place all in a *large* bowl.

3 bananas, sliced
3 medium to large apples, diced
3 oranges, diced
1 can pineapple pieces and natural juices
1 can unsweetened bing cherries and juice
1 bunch grapes (your choice)
1 grapefruit, diced

Mix all this fruit together and chill. As you serve you may want to add a few miniature marshmallows to each serving.

This salad is delicious and refreshing and a perfect ending to any meal or snack.

If it is too tart for you sweet-toothed people, you may add a touch of sugar.

Matador Ranch, Texas. 1908. *The Matador chuck wagon in West pasture.*

Git Along Little Dogies,
My Dinner's Gittin' Cold

Now you all may or may not have heard of the Iowa winters but let me tell you, as I am originally a good old southern hoosier, my first winter spent in Iowa was a definite shocker!

I was working on this new cattle ranch in Iowa and we had come through the winter pretty good without losing many cows and calves. Although a few times I thought I might have lost a toe or finger or two due to frostbite and had half my hide torn to shreds by those "man-eating" thorn trees that grow in abundance in the Midwest. I'm telling you those trees have thorns sometimes three to four inches long and they just seem to reach out and grab you no matter where you are in the pasture.

I thought I had finally adjusted to those 70–90 mph winds, dangerously cold temperature, and hazards of the land and I was feeling pretty proud. Then all hell broke loose! I woke up one morning in April and the snow was flying. We cowboys are like the mailman—neither snow, sleet nor rain keeps us from our duty—I donned several layers of clothes and headed out to the barn to saddle up. All the ranch hands showed up at about the same time and were grumbling about the snow and wind. We were soon assigned to our areas and rode off to find and round up as many cows and newborn calves as we could and get them to safety.

I found several newborn calves and herded them along with their mothers to safety and shelter. Now cows are kinda funny and they don't know when you're trying to help them. They always seem to want to go the opposite way of where you want them to go and even during a storm it isn't any different. I had a battle on my hands getting them grouped and moved to the safety of the wooded area on high ground. Then there was this dumb cow bawling and standing half way down a river bank. I couldn't get her to move from that spot and finally realized why. She had calved, of all places, down at the bottom of the river bank. Her calf was half sunk in the mud and couldn't get out! Since the wind had picked up to about 70 mph, throwing a rope was impossible. My only choice was to dally my rope on the saddle, hang on and climb down the bank. This was done very slowly due to the thigh deep snow already piled on the bank side. Of course when I reached the calf, it didn't want to cooperate and had to be persuaded to let me secure the loop around its middle. This done, I climbed back up and had Ol' Buck, my horse, back up and soon the calf's body flipped over the top of the bank. Momma cow ran over and began to lick it and make sure it was hers and shield it from the storm. While taking the pair to the bunch in the wooded area, poor Ol' Buck just seemed to go clear out from under me! When I looked down, all I could see was one ear and a whole bunch of snow but I could still feel him. I hung on for dear life and kicked his sides and after three lunges we made it out of the snow bank! After this I decided those cows could fend for themselves and I was heading home!

As I got back to the barn I discovered several others had the same idea. After stabling our mounts we climbed into our four wheel drives and headed home where another surprise awaited me. Across my drive was a 20 foot wide snow drift and it looked damn near that deep! This was not going to keep me from a warm fire and a fantastic dinner of homemade vegetable soup and hot biscuits! Not when I could almost taste them and be warmed clear down to my toes just by the thought.

I pulled my truck over to the side, parked it, pulled my boots up higher and set out to climb that wall of snow! I stopped right on the top and looked around as far as I could see, which wasn't very far due to the flying snow, and I had to agree with them romantic writers and poets—it was a beautiful, wild sight!

COOKIN' FOR A CROWD

During the summer we like to cook out and have friends over. Well, I would have trouble figuring how much to cook so I spent some time watching our guests to see how much they eat and this is what I came up with—they eat a bunch! I created a guideline for chuck wagon cookin' based on twenty-five people.

FOOD	QUANTITY
Wieners	6½ lbs.
Hamburger	10 lbs.
Sliced ham	12 lbs.
Chicken	16 lbs.
Fish (whole)	15 lbs.
Fish patties	8 lbs.
Potato salad	5 quarts
Baked beans	3 quarts
Bread	3 1 lb. loaves
Butter	½ lb.
Coffee	2 gallons
Iced Tea	3½ gallons
Lemonade	2 gallons
Watermelon	45 lbs.
Ice Cream	3 gallons
Beer	I don't know your friends but I do know mine. I have them bring their own—it's cheaper!!!

Chow time under the noonday sun.

INDEX